ALIEN

INVESTIGATION

SEARCHING FOR THE TRUTH ABOUT UFOs AND ALIENS

KELLY MILNER HALLS

Illustrated by **RICK C. SPEARS**

DEDICATION

This book is dedicated to my mom, who always said I was her little alien;
to my dad who knows about space; to my heavenly daughters Kerry and
Vanessa; and to a few reading stars—you know who you are—from McKinley
Elementary in Yakima, Washington. It's also dedicated to my best friend, who
taught me to hope for new worlds of my own.

ACKNOWLEDGMENT

This book would not have been possible without the generous assistance of
the Mutual UFO Network (MUFON) and the staff of their 2010 Symposium in
Denver, Colorado. Their lectures and my subsequent interviews of their experts
helped bring the topic and the possibilities into focus, and I'm grateful to Clifford
Clift, John Greenewald, Stanton Friedman, Kevin D. Randle, and Michael Schratt
in particular. I'm also grateful to my editor, Carol Hinz, and illustrator, Rick
Spears. You brought this project to life.

Millbrook Press
A division of Lerner Publishing Group, Inc.
241 First Avenue North
Minneapolis, MN 55401 U.S.A.

Website address: www.lernerbooks.com

Main body text set in Adobe Jenson Pro 14/22. Typeface provided by Adobe Systems.

Library of Congress Cataloging-in-Publication Data

Halls, Kelly Milner, 1957–
    Alien investigation : searching for the truth about UFOs and aliens / by Kelly Milner
  Halls ; illustrated by Rick C. Spears.
       p.   cm.
    Includes bibliographical references and index.
    ISBN: 978–0–7613–6204–3 (lib. bdg. : alk. paper)
    1. Unidentified flying objects—Juvenile literature. 2. Extraterrestrial beings—Juvenile
  literature. I. Spears, Rick. II. Title.
  TL789.2.H35 2012
  001.942—dc23   2011022230

Manufactured in the United States of America
1 — BC — 12/31/11

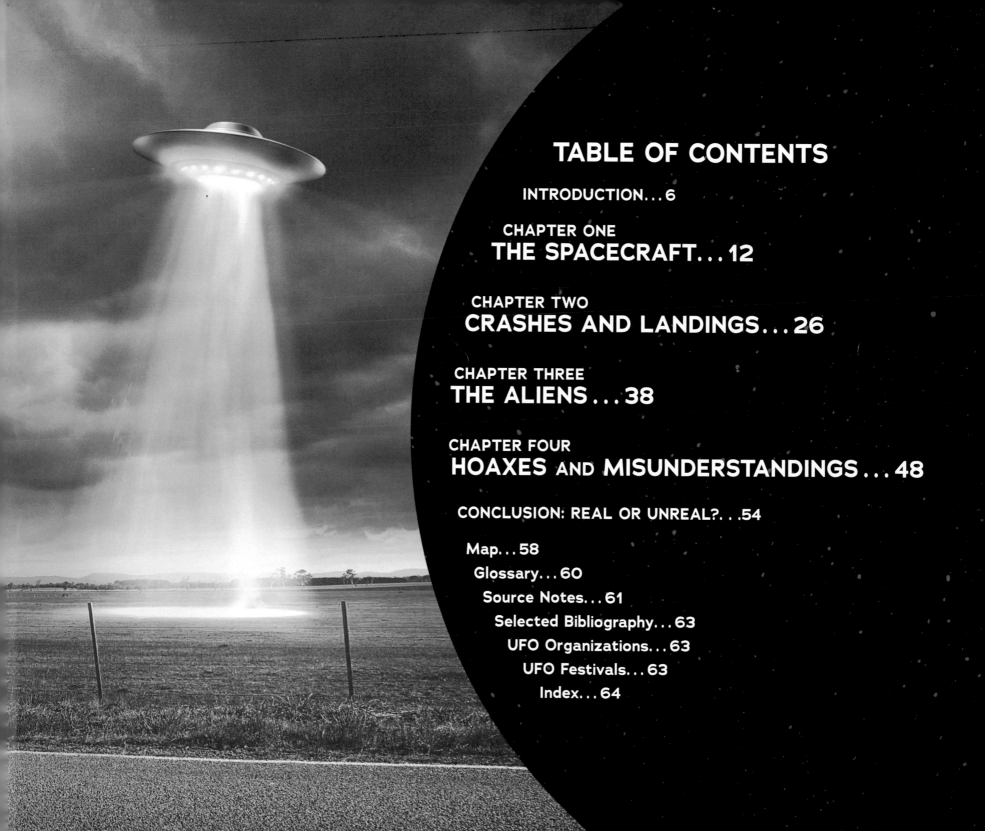

TABLE OF CONTENTS

IMAGINE... a team of bold explorers as they prepare to leave their home planet. The leader, Yllek, wonders, "Could the alien species be real?" That question fuels their mission. They plan to observe a distant blue planet. The journey could be dangerous, but the desire to expand the reach of science compels the team. They carefully prepare and hope they will make it to Earth—and back home again.

INTRODUCTION

As a kid, I lived near Houston, Texas. My father was a computer expert at the Johnson Space Center, a part of the National Aeronautics and Space Administration (NASA). I loved the stories and pictures he brought home about manned space missions. It sounds wrong to say "manned space missions" when men and women can both be astronauts. But people weren't talking about the gender of the crew then. They were marking the difference between missions with human crew members and missions without them—manned or unmanned. When each rocket was prepped for launch, we gathered around the television to watch.

Success was uncertain in those early years. Missions were sometimes scrubbed, or canceled at the last minute. Accidents happened. When Virgil "Gus" Grissom, Edward White, and Roger Chaffee died in a launchpad fire while preparing for the first Apollo mission on January 27, 1967, my father cried.

I loved watching science-fiction television shows such as *Star Trek* and *The Outer Limits*. I began to wonder: Could other planets have astronauts of their own? Could they fly from their planets to visit ours?

Some people believe the answer to these questions is yes. They believe in unidentified flying objects (UFO). Thousands say they have seen UFOs. Others describe face-to-face alien encounters.

Apollo 4 (left) was successfully launched on November 9, 1967. Earlier that year, three astronauts *(center)* died in a fire on the launchpad. Space exploration inspired fictional television shows, such as *Star Trek (right)*.

Physicist Stanton Friedman worked for high-tech corporations including General Electric, General Motors, and McDonnell Douglas for many years. But in 1958, an interest in UFOs took root. Since that time, Friedman has studied and written about the scientific likelihood of extraterrestrial visitors.

Do the laws of physics allow for the possibility of long-distance space travel?

The laws of physics have nothing to do with the possibility of flight to nearby or distant stars. There are roughly two thousand stars within only 55 light-years of Earth. [One light-year is equal to 6 trillion miles (9.7 trillion kilometers).] About 5 percent are similar to the sun, and some are a billion or more years older than the sun. The key [to traveling to the stars] is the development of advanced technology. [And that] requires lots of money, talented people, and time.

A person couldn't fly from New York, New York, to San Francisco, California, in 1900 because the technology for flight hadn't been developed, not because [it was against] the laws of physics. We did learn a lot along the way. Some people think that because physicist Albert Einstein said things can't go faster than the speed of light, the minimum round-trip time for a journey to a star 40 light-years away would be eighty years. Not true. Einstein also said time slows down for things moving close to the speed of light. At only 99.99 percent of the speed of light, one could go 37 light-years in six months. So yes, transportation to the stars is feasible.

Is it possible that life-forms on other planets have technology more advanced than our technology on Earth?

It is not only possible but very likely because our technology is so new compared to technology on a planet that's been around 4.5 billion years longer. And there is overwhelming evidence that Earth is being visited by intelligently controlled high-performance vehicles.

Why is it important for us to study UFOs scientifically?

We will learn more about the local galactic neighborhood, about new means of propulsion, about the variety of inhabited worlds out there, about how unimportant we are in the larger scheme of things.

Artists' depictions of an alien *(above)* and a UFO *(left)*

9

Are UFOs and aliens real? We'll explore possible answers in this book. But keep a few things in mind as you read.

We can't always answer who, what, where, and why when it comes to some UFOs. But we can gather evidence and seek out expert analysis. Thanks to eyewitness reports, we can consider the scientific possibilities and come to our own conclusions.

Will you believe in aliens and UFOs as the book ends? It's hard to tell. But if you're inspired to ask more questions and seek more answers, the world—even the universe—will be a better place. The next great discovery could be yours.

IMAGINE… a gigantic hanger filled with dozens of ships. Yllek inspects each craft, calculating which one will give his team the best chance of success. They may need the stealth of a saucer or the blinding speed of an orb. But for traveling such a great distance, he concludes, they'll need the mother ship—a home away from home to transport them to the strange world they'll be exploring. Smaller shuttles will ferry them to the surface once they arrive.

CHAPTER ONE:

THE
SPACECRAFT

To understand UFOs and the people
who study them, start with the basics.
What have people claimed to see? Do
UFO descriptions differ from person to
person? Do the witnesses seem reliable?
This chapter offers a short history of UFO
sightings. It also introduces the different
UFO shapes described by witnesses. It
includes one story per decade starting
with the first UFO report filed with the
U.S. military in 1947.

Discs and Saucers
1947—Near Mineral, Washington

On June 24, 1947, Idaho businessman and rescue pilot Kenneth Arnold was flying to Yakima, Washington. He was searching for a lost aircraft worth $5,000 in reward money when he saw something unexpected. Nine disc-shaped unidentified objects were flying over Mount Rainier. Each was about the size of a DC-4 airplane. These planes are 94 feet (29 meters) long and 118 feet (36 m) wide. Arnold said the objects were fast, agile, and unlike anything he'd seen before.

How fast? Arnold's calculations suggested the UFOs cut through the air at speeds nearing 1,700 miles (2,700 km) per hour. That was three times faster than any known manned aircraft flying in 1947. A prospector named Fred Johnson said he saw six flying objects above him from the ground at the same day, time, and approximate location as Arnold reported.

Reporters from the *Pendleton (Oregon) East Oregonian* newspaper interviewed Arnold on June 25, 1947. After the story was published, at least fifteen other witnesses from the state of Washington came forward.

The news coverage of the sighting included what was probably the first reference to flying saucers. When describing his experience to reporters, Arnold said the objects "flew erratic, like a saucer if you skip it across the water."

On July 4, 1947, United Airlines pilot E. J. Smith and his copilot saw five to nine disc-shaped objects over Idaho. Arnold and Smith later met, compared notes, and agreed they had experienced nearly identical sightings. Together, they filed official reports with the U.S. Army Air Force. These were the first UFO reports filed with the military.

In the decades since the sighting near Mineral, hundreds of other sightings have made the saucer- or disc-shaped UFOs one of the most common shapes on record.

The Flying Saucer as I Saw it... by Kenneth Arnold
Per copy 50¢

This image shows the drawing that Kenneth Arnold *(inset)* made after his UFO sighting in 1947.

Spheres and Ovoids 1952—Washington, D.C.

Shining lights, appearing as either spheres or ovoids (egg-shaped objects) were documented in Washington, D.C., in July 1952. According to UFO expert Richard H. Hall, "The summer 1952 UFO sighting wave was one of the largest of all time, and arguably the most significant of all time in terms of the credible reports and hardcore scientific data obtained." Dozens of people saw the balls of light, for several nights.

Just before midnight on July 19, air traffic controller Edward Nugent spotted seven mysterious objects on his radar screen. He was just 15 miles (24 km) from downtown Washington, D.C. A controller at the airport's other radar center, Howard Cocklin, reported he could see one of the crafts on his radar and through his control tower window. Cocklin described it as "a bright orange light."

The objects seemed to average a speed of 100 miles (160 km) per hour. Several F-94 fighter jets were quickly sent to investigate the objects but were easily outrun. Estimates suggest the UFOs topped 7,000 miles (11,300 km) per hour when accelerating.

Local newspapers and national publications including *Life Magazine* reported that "Unidentified Aerial Objects" had been seen over the U.S. Capitol Building. The articles included photographs of the objects as well. A military memo dated July 28, 1952, said Washington National Airport tower controllers had picked up objects on their scopes. The memo confirmed that controllers at Andrews Air Force Base had also "made contact."

Air traffic controllers in Arlington, Virginia, not long after the July 1952 UFO sighting wave

The objects returned on July 26 and 27. A squadron of F-94 fighters was scrambled (quickly sent up) to pursue them but was unsuccessful. "They've surrounded my plane," one pilot reported. "What should I do?" Eventually, the objects took evasive action and disappeared.

On July 29, air force officials held a press conference to discuss the sightings. They blamed a weather phenomenon known as temperature inversions for the balls of light. They said cool air trapped below warm air created flat cloud formations, which people mistook for UFOs. The government's Project Blue Book investigators—experts asked to explain UFO sightings—later retracted the explanation and listed the series of sightings as officially unexplained.

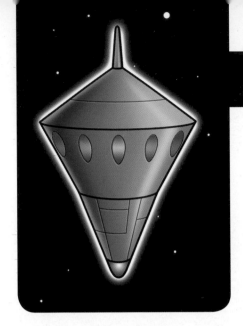

Forty-five-year-old hunter James W. Flynn was walking his dogs in the Florida Everglades just after midnight on March 15, 1965. He spotted a bright light descending roughly 1 mile (1.6 km) away. He thought the light might be from a downed helicopter or experimental aircraft from Cape Kennedy (now known as Cape Canaveral Air Force Station). So he caged his dogs, put them on his swamp buggy, and sped toward the light to offer assistance.

As he neared the mysterious glow, he stopped his vehicle and continued on foot through the shallows. Flynn's dogs howled within their cages on the boat, disturbed by the sound coming from the object, a noise similar to a diesel generator.

As Flynn broke through the trees, he found the source of the light. It was unlike anything he'd seen before. A cone-shaped craft roughly 75 feet (23 m) wide and 30 feet (9 m) high hovered about 3 feet (1 m) from the ground. Several rows of porthole windows emitted yellow light, but Flynn couldn't see inside the craft.

Cautiously, he inched closer, waving his arms in a friendly gesture. A thin beam of blue light burst silently from the mysterious craft and struck him in the forehead, knocking him unconscious. "I felt a blow like a sledgehammer between the eyes," Flynn told the

The Florida Everglades in the mid-1900s

Cape Canaveral Air Force Station in 1965

Fort Myers News-Press three days after the ordeal. "That's all I know."

Hours later, Flynn woke alone with a painful bruise where the beam had hit him. His vision and hearing were also temporarily impaired. The craft had vanished, leaving a 72-foot (22 m) scorched circle on the ground and blackened treetops.

Officials from the Homestead Air Force Base interviewed Flynn during his stay in a Fort Meyers hospital. Those officials later called his story a hoax. But representatives from the National Investigations Committee on Aerial Phenomena (NICAP) also spoke with Flynn. The NICAP said his experience might be real, noting the physical evidence left behind.

Doctors confirmed Flynn's wounds could not have been self-inflicted. And the NICAP said there were no footprints found around the large charred circle, suggesting Flynn had not burned the ground himself.

Rectangular 1976—Tehran, Iran

In the early hours of September 19, 1976, multiple reports of a UFO poured in to authorities at the Imperial Iranian Air Force command post. Assistant Deputy Commander of Operations Nadar Yousefi first wondered if citizens were mistaking the planet Venus for an aircraft. But after he saw the UFO, he scrambled an F-4 fighter jet from Shahrokhi Air Force Base to investigate.

The planet Venus *(right)*, as seen from Earth, is twenty times brighter than the brightest star in the sky.

The pilot left the base at one thirty in the morning to journey 70 miles (113 km) north to the object's location. Halfway to its destination, the F-4 began to malfunction. First, the communications equipment stopped working. Then other important electronic elements failed. The pilot had no choice but to head back toward the base. Almost immediately, the plane began to operate normally again.

A second F-4 got closer to the UFO. Its radar confirmed the craft was as large as a commercial airliner. The shape was unclear due to the brilliant glow of the red, blue, green, and orange lights. But the pattern of the lights suggested it might be rectangular.

As the jet closed in, the UFO suddenly darted away, surpassing the F-4's top speed. From a distance, the F-4 crew members saw a second object drop from the mother ship and shoot toward them. The crew locked onto its target and tried to fire its AIM-9 missile. The missile was unresponsive.

Faced with a head-on collision with a UFO, the F-4 crew took evasive action and retreated. The smaller craft tailed the F-4 for a short time and then rejoined the mother ship. Once the F-4 was headed back toward the base, all controls were once again functional. To this day, the exchange remains unexplained.

This F-4 fighter plane is the same type that was sent after the mysterious UFO.

Belinda Perdew Taylor is a well-respected children's librarian at a Kentucky elementary school. But as a teenager, she had a series of encounters she still can't explain.

How old were you when you had your UFO experience?

I was nineteen years old.

Where were you?

I was driving east down Highway 44, from Mount Washington, Kentucky, on my way home to Shepherdsville. There were no lights along the side of the highway—just a dark, two-lane road.

What happened?

I started back around 11:30 P.M. I was halfway home when I saw the most incredible sight. Three very luminous chandelier-like shapes were hovering right in front of me as I drove.

Because it was July, I thought at first it might be fireworks. But it didn't take long to realize whatever was looming in front of me was not fireworks. No matter how fast I drove, and believe me, I was driving fast, the three vessels stayed right in front of my windshield.

What happened when you got home?

I ran straight upstairs to my parents' bedroom. My mother, who was awake by this time, asked me what was wrong.

"Do you believe in UFOs?" I asked.

My mother replied, "I think there is a great big universe out there and we may not be the only things living in it." I was speechless. I just felt better that one of the most important people in my life didn't think I was being foolish.

Was that the last time you saw the UFOs?

No. I saw them several nights in a row. I stopped meeting my friends to avoid driving on Highway 44 at night. But the "chandelier spaceships" popped up on my street every night for at least three, maybe four nights after the initial sighting on the highway.

Did anyone else ever see them?

My best friend Becky and I met at my house nearly every evening to walk our dogs. That's when she saw them too.

When I looked up that night and saw the spaceships, I reached for Becky's hand and whispered, "Do you see them?" She confirmed that she did, and she had no idea what they were. We both decided to go back home.

Have you seen a UFO since then?

I've never had another experience like that one. However, I do know my Uncle Sam had a very similar experience and he was right around the same age. He doesn't talk about it.

Triangles and Boomerangs 1997–Phoenix, Arizona

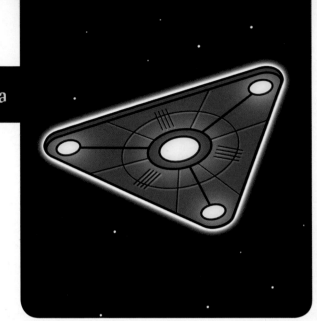

On February 6, 1995, Phoenix medical doctor and television personality Lynne D. Kitei saw something strange from her bedroom window. Three bright amber lights were hovering 50 to 75 feet (15 to 23 m) from the ground less than 100 yards (91 m) from her property.

As Kitei ran to grab her camera, one of the three lights faded to black, "as though it were being controlled by a dimmer switch," she said. She missed capturing all three lights that first night, but she did snap a series of pictures of the two remaining orbs before they also disappeared.

Almost two years later, on January 22, 1997, the amber orbs returned. This time, they were farther away and higher in the sky. Once again, the lights soon faded. On January 23, they returned. Kitei was prepared, her video camera in hand. After she captured seventeen seconds of footage, the camcorder batteries died. Later that night, six amber lights returned and faded.

Kitei was determined to discover what the orbs were. She called the local newspaper and the nearby Luke Air Force Base. She wanted to know if anyone else had seen the lights and if there was a logical explanation. Unsatisfied with the answers she received, Kitei contacted air traffic controllers at Sky Harbor International Airport. They had seen the lights but had no explanation.

USA Today published this image in 1997. The newspaper reported that people saw something like this V-shaped object flying over Arizona for 106 minutes on March 13.

Thousands of witnesses joined Kitei in her search for answers soon after. On March 13, 1997, many Phoenix residents saw glowing lights. The Mutual UFO Network (MUFON) took reports from a number of observers.

"It was bigger than anything I had ever seen in the sky before or since," one report said. "It was a boomerang shape with lights at each point. The lights were bright like baseball field lights. Everybody stood there silent just staring with the occasional 'What is that?' being muttered.

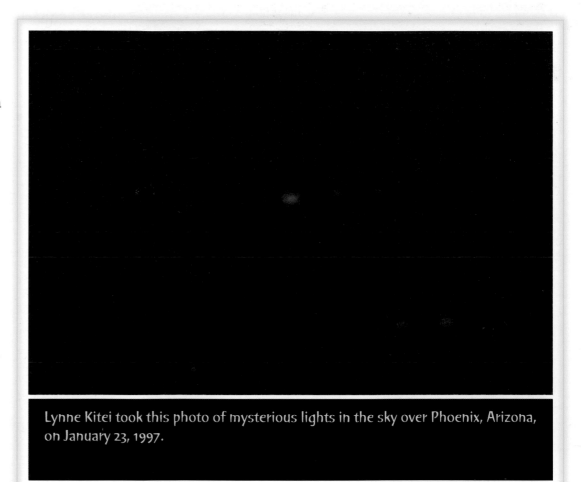

Lynne Kitei took this photo of mysterious lights in the sky over Phoenix, Arizona, on January 23, 1997.

"I am not a rocket scientist," the report continued, "but anything the length of two or more football fields that propels itself through the air should at the very least make some sort of sound. But there was nothing."

Magazines, newspapers, and news programs across the nation reported on the strange lights. The event became known as Phoenix Lights. On July 25, 1997, the U.S. Air Force said the light show witnessed by people in Phoenix was not a UFO. It was the Maryland National Guard dropping flares from an A-10 Warthog aircraft on the Barry Goldwater Range. The southwest Arizona range is used for bombing practice by the U.S. Air Force and Marine Corps.

In a 2004 demonstration, an S-3B Viking releases flares over the Atlantic Ocean.

Kitei and other witnesses insisted they'd seen flares before and these were not flares. Flares were lights that faded as they fizzled and fell to the ground.

In March 2007, almost ten years to the day from the original Phoenix Lights, the lights returned. This time, local television news crews captured the lights on film. Former Arizona governor Fife Symington, who had witnessed the lights in 1997, came forward to say he believed the lights were an "otherworldly" UFO.

"I'm a pilot and I know just about every machine that flies," Symington said. "It was bigger than anything I've ever seen. It remains a great mystery. Other people saw it, responsible people. I don't know why people would ridicule it."

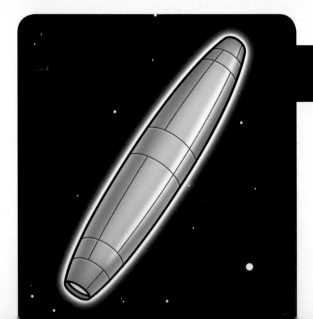

Cylinders 2010—Hangzhou, China

Air traffic screeched to a halt for an hour over Hangzhou, China, on the evening of July 7, 2010. Witnesses reported seeing a cigar-shaped UFO with a "bright comet-like tail." Hangzhou Xioshan International Airport grounded or rerouted all flights after nine in the evening, delaying twenty flights and up to two thousand passengers.

Crew members of commercial airlines were the first to see the UFO. Hundreds of Chinese citizens on the ground spotted it as well.

"The thing suddenly ran westwards fast, like it was escaping from something," said a bus driver in the region. Other residents said it radiated bursts of red and white light.

Some aviation experts theorized a private plane was responsible for the disruption. But Wang Jian, head of air traffic control at the Zhejiang branch of China's Civil Aviation Administration, said no firm conclusions had been drawn. Chinese regulations make such incidents unlikely.

By July 26, the Beijing UFO Research Organization (BURO) said there was no evidence the sighting was "associated with an extraterrestrial flying saucer." However, it noted that Chinese radar had not detected anything. According to BURO, airport radar has a problem with blind spots.

Chinese aviation officials refused to release photos or videos of the strange object. They claimed the images ordinary citizens shared were not connected to the airport incident. But eyewitnesses remain unconvinced.

Hangzhou Xioshan International Airport is in eastern China. Hangzhou is the capital city of Zhejiang Province.

By day Michael Schratt is an aerospace draftsman in Tempe, Arizona. But in his spare time, he is a pilot, historian, and expert on something called black programs. Those are top secret projects world governments prefer to keep top secret. For years he's searched for clues about experimental aircraft, which are often mistaken for UFOs. Most people are not allowed to see the aircraft. But someone has to build, fuel, and fly the secret machines. Schratt gathers every scrap of evidence he can find—every interview, every article, and every secret revealed. He shares what he learns with others who are interested in the subject.

"I believe that some UFOs are extraterrestrial spacecraft," he says, meaning flying vehicles from other worlds. But he believes that many reports are actually sightings of top secret projects.

How many experimental planes are built and tested in the United States each year?

Technically, nobody within the civilian (nonmilitary) community knows. However, a reasonable number, including manned and unmanned aircraft programs, is approximately four per year.

How often would you estimate UFO sightings are actually top secret aviation projects?

It's my personal belief that 95 percent of what people report as extraterrestrial UFOs are, in point of fact, classified aircraft programs developed within the American aerospace industry.

Is it possible some secret crafts are based on information gathered from actual UFOs that our government has recovered and hidden?

The possibility exists that some American aerospace programs were influenced by extraterrestrial vehicles recovered from 1941 to 1970. However, physical evidence or documentation to confirm this has not been made available to the general public.

Would the average person be amazed by what top secret aircraft can do?

Yes, absolutely. Reference the comment made by the former head of Lockheed Skunk Works, Ben Rich. [Lockheed is famous for building both top secret and traditional aircraft.] He said, "We have things in the desert that are fifty years beyond what you can dream of. If you've seen it on *Star Wars* or *Star Trek*, we've been there, done that, or decided it wasn't worth the effort."

IMAGINE... THE EXPLORERS HAVE REACHED THEIR DESTINATION. YLLEK HAS PUT HIS SECOND-IN-COMMAND IN CHARGE OF THE MOTHER SHIP. HE AND TWO OTHERS ARE NOW SPEEDING TOWARD THE PLANET IN A SHUTTLE CRAFT. THEY ENGAGE THEIR SILENT ENGINES, DIM THEIR INTERNAL LIGHTS, AND SEARCH FOR A SAFE PLACE TO TOUCH DOWN. "OUR MISSION IS TO COLLECT DATA," HE REMINDS HIS CREW. "IF THERE ARE LIFE-FORMS ON THIS PLANET, IT WOULD BE WISE TO AVOID DETECTION." WISE, PERHAPS. BUT AVOIDING DETECTION MAY BE HARDER THAN THEY THINK.

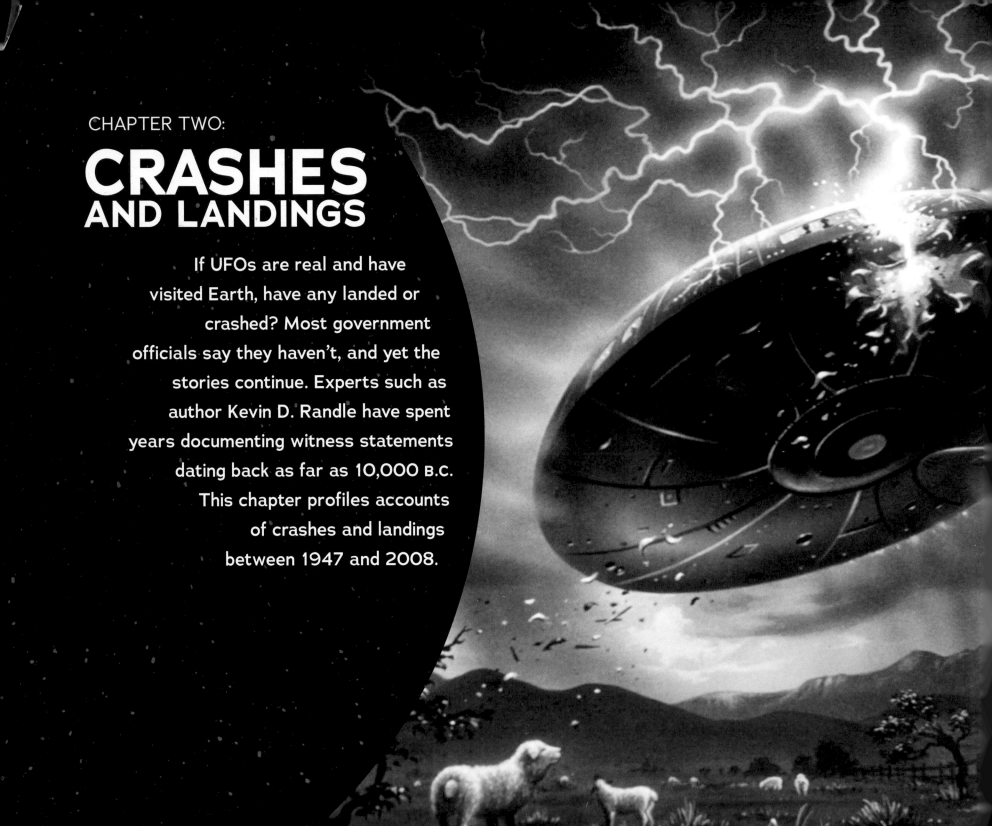

CHAPTER TWO:

CRASHES
AND LANDINGS

If UFOs are real and have visited Earth, have any landed or crashed? Most government officials say they haven't, and yet the stories continue. Experts such as author Kevin D. Randle have spent years documenting witness statements dating back as far as 10,000 B.C. This chapter profiles accounts of crashes and landings between 1947 and 2008.

in son... ...and the public mains on political and
history, what... "newsworthy" has met dif- ever, the news media
has considered "newsworthy" has met dif-
ferent definitions. For example, mid-twen-

CRASH: ROSWELL, NEW MEXICO—1947

In the summer of 1947, just days after Kenneth Arnold spotted a string of nine UFOs over western Washington, the skies of New Mexico came alive with thunder and lightning. With the storm, reports said, came a string of unexplained activities. Rumors began to swirl. Had a mysterious object fallen to Earth in the early hours of July 2, 1947?

Foster Ranch foreman William "Mac" Brazel carried scraps of strange debris to Roswell sheriff George M. Wilcox on July 6 or 7. He'd found the debris on the ranch he was paid to oversee, and much more was still at the ranch.

Puzzled by the odd material, Wilcox called officials at the Roswell Army Air Field (RAAF). Major Jesse Marcel's team was sent to investigate. Brazel escorted them to the ranch, and they gathered the remaining material. Marcel loaded one box into his car and headed back to Roswell. But before he checked in at the base, he made a midnight stop at home.

Marcel woke his wife and eleven-year-old son Jesse Marcel Jr. He poured the debris on the kitchen floor and urged his sleepy family to examine each strange piece. He told them to pay special attention to any pieces that might have electrical parts. He also asked them to piece them together like a jigsaw puzzle, if they could.

Jesse Jr. tried hard to follow the instructions, but the pieces didn't fit together. He found nothing that looked like a transistor or wire. The silver debris was light and sturdy, almost impossible to break or even crinkle. It would not burn, and pieces would return to their original shape after being crumpled. Some pieces were smooth. Others were etched with strange markings. Every scrap seemed totally unfamiliar. Jesse Jr. agreed with his father when he said the pieces were "nothing made on this earth."

The RAAF seemed to agree when it issued a press release on July 8. "The many rumors regarding the flying disc became a reality yesterday," the release read. "The intelligence office of the 509th Bomb Group of the Eighth Air Force, Roswell Army Air Field, was fortunate enough to gain possession of a disc through the cooperation of one of the local ranchers and the sheriff's office of Chaves County."

The *Roswell Daily Record*'s headline said, "RAAF Captures Flying Saucer." Other newspapers also carried the report. But by July 9, the RAAF had issued a retraction. The army insisted it was a weather balloon—a large, inflated balloon used to collect weather data high in the atmosphere. The army tried to put the controversy to rest.

Major Jesse Marcel with debris that the army claims came from a weather balloon

Jesse Marcel Sr. died in 1986, but his son, Jesse Marcel Jr., followed in his father's footsteps. Marcel Jr. has spent his life in military service, including as an officer in Iraq. He has also been a medical doctor in the United States and abroad. He shares his memories of handling debris from the Roswell, New Mexico, crash with us here.

What do you remember most vividly about the debris your father brought home in 1947?

My most vivid remembrance of the debris [was] the symbols imprinted on the inner edge of the beams. I recall them as at first looking like Egyptian hieroglyphics, but on closer examination, they were geometric symbols, i.e., oblate spheroids, truncated triangles, circles, etc., that were of a violet hue—semi-reflective of light.

Was it hard not to tell your friends about what you'd seen?

Actually my dad came in shortly after getting back from General Ramey's office and sat my mother and me down and sternly told us NOT to talk about it. And no, I didn't talk about it.

You have said that your father was excited and fascinated by the debris. Were you excited too? Or were you afraid?

At first, after going to the kitchen where the debris was spread out, I failed to appreciate the moment until my dad's excitement caught on and I started looking at the debris. His statement in so many words said this was part of a flying saucer—not really realizing what it was, but after looking at it and recognizing the unusual quality of the debris, I started getting excited too. No fear involved.

If you could go back in time to examine the material, what would you do differently?

It would have been very tempting to keep a sample of the debris, but being an army air force brat [child of a parent in the air force], I would not have. I would have dug out my camera and taken pictures though.

What would you like to share with kids about what you've learned since that day?

I would like to confirm that we are not alone and that they are probably scientists from another world interested in our civilization. There is no evidence that they mean us harm. I have to add that this has increased my belief in God.

The army released photos of Marcel with the debris. Some people said they were staged pictures with weather balloons replacing the real debris. Some said they were proof the UFO was real. Either way, Lieutenant General Roger M. Ramey instructed Marcel and others never to discuss the details again.

For decades the crash did not receive much attention. Then, in the late 1970s and the 1980s, writers including Stanton T. Friedman and Kevin D. Randle became interested in learning more. They interviewed Jesse Marcel Sr. and hundreds of others who discounted the weather balloon story. According to the research, there were two crash sites—one on the Foster Ranch and one closer to Corona, New Mexico, than Roswell. Some witnesses say that alien bodies were also found with the UFO debris. You'll find more about this possibility in the next chapter. Roswell remains the most famous UFO crash report of all time.

LANDINGS: LEVELLAND, TEXAS—1957

A bizarre phone call came in to Officer A. J. Fowler the night of November 2, 1957, at the Levelland, Texas, police department. Pedro Saucedo and Joe Salaz had seen a bright flash of blue light 4 miles (6 km) west of Levelland. A strange torpedo-shaped craft approached their truck. At that moment, the truck's headlights and the engine failed. Once the craft flew away, the engine started as it normally would.

"I jumped out of the truck and hit the dirt because I was afraid," Saucedo said. "The thing passed directly over my truck with a great sound and a rush of wind. It sounded like thunder and my truck rocked from the blast. I felt a lot of heat. Then I got up and watched it go."

Fowler passed that first call off as a joke. But a second call came in an hour later. About 4 miles (6.4 km) east of Levelland, Jim Wheeler reported an egg-shaped craft bathed in blue light blocking the road. His engine died as he approached the object but restarted once it took flight.

More than nine other witnesses saw the craft in the hours that followed. They described it as being between 100 and 200 feet (30 and 60 m) long. National press coverage and a rash of other regional sightings soon followed. For days, citizens in Texas and New Mexico spotted similar crafts.

One New Mexico newspaper reported that "two Hobbs men, who refused to permit use of their names said the strange light stalled their cars even though they tried to outrun it at speeds up to 90 mph [145 km per hour]."

An artist's rendering of ball lightning. Some authorities have said UFO sightings are actually ball lightning.

Hobbs is roughly 100 miles (160 km) southwest of Levelland.

Agents from the U.S. Air Force's Project Blue Book—a task force formed in 1951 to investigate UFO reports—interviewed Saucedo and Salaz. They suggested that area thunderstorms and ball lightning had caused the electrical disruptions.

What is ball lightning? Scientists aren't certain because it is so rare. But they think it's a ball of energy suspended in midair, often during thunderstorms. It can sometimes appear during calmer weather as well. Ball lightning looks like a glowing ball of light with fuzzy edges. It may be less than 1 inch (2.5 centimeters) across or as large as 3 feet (1 m) across.

Case closed, according to the U.S. Air Force. But several scientists including James McDonald of the University of Arizona and J. Allen Hynek of Northwestern University disputed the air force's claim. After careful analysis of the eyewitness reports and regional weather conditions, these scientists confirmed there was no electrical storm during the Levelland sighting.

31

CRASH: KECKSBURG, PENNSYLVANIA—1965

Thousands saw the brilliant fireball streak across northeastern skies at a quarter to five in the evening on December 9, 1965. Regional pilots submitted more than twenty official reports about it to the Federal Aviation Administration. Metallic debris fell on several states, including Ohio and Michigan. In Kecksburg, Pennsylvania, 30 miles (48 km) from Pittsburgh, witnesses said the object hit the ground.

By six thirty, Kecksburg resident Frances Kalp was on the phone with reporter John Murphy of radio station WHJB in Greensburg, Pennsylvania. Kalp described a smoldering craft the size of a VW Beetle that looked to her like a fiery "four pointed star." Murphy drove to Kecksburg to investigate.

Two officers were at the forest crash site by the time Murphy arrived. When he asked if anything had landed in the wooded location, police said he would have to speak with the military. Murphy later went to a Pennsylvania State Police barrack for a briefing with Captain Joseph Dussia. But by the time Murphy arrived, plans had changed.

"The Pennsylvania State Police have made a thorough search of the woods," Dussia said. "We are convinced there is nothing whatsoever in the woods."

Denied access to the woods, Murphy couldn't see the craft for himself. But other witnesses shared their stories. Volunteer firefighter Jim Romansky had been at the crash site before the military arrived. He said he saw an acorn-shaped object 9 to 12 feet (2.7 to 3.7 m) in diameter with a golden band around the bottom. Symbols resembling Egyptian hieroglyphs were etched on the band.

Witness Bill Bulebush *(left)* and UFO expert Stan Gordon near a model of the object that crashed in Kecksburg, Pennsylvania, in 1965

Russian workmen with a model of a Soviet satellite

Years later, NASA claimed the crash was part of a fallen Soviet satellite—an explanation it had strongly denied just days after the original report. Other scientists said it was a blazing meteor, which is certainly possible. Whatever it actually was, local witnesses say a military flatbed truck left the wooded crash location with something large strapped securely in place, tarps shielding it from view.

LANDING: RENDLESHAM FOREST, UNITED KINGDOM—1980

In the early morning of December 26, 1980, twenty-year-old Airman John Burroughs was on patrol at the Royal Air Force (RAF) Woodbridge station. The base was near Rendlesham Forest and the RAF Bentwaters base. U.S. Air Force troops were using both bases. Burroughs was driving a familiar path at three in the morning when he spotted something in the distance: a weird glow coming from blinking colored lights. He immediately returned to base to make a report.

Staff Sergeant James Penniston was concerned the lights might be from a downed aircraft. He and Burroughs headed back to the forest to investigate further. When they couldn't drive any closer, they continued on foot. They remained in walkie-talkie communications with the base until Penniston felt an electric charge in the air. Static suddenly overtook the radio signals.

In a clearing, the men saw a bright light coming from a strange object. As Penniston came within 10 feet (3 m) of it, the light dimmed slightly. There was no smell of smoke and no sign of a crash.

"I'm a rational person," Penniston said in a History Channel documentary. "But I could not come up with a rational explanation."

What he could do was write down notes and take photos. The object was triangular and about 9 feet (2.7 m) wide and 6.5 feet (2 m) high. It had no obvious front or back, no windows or doors, and no landing gear. The object made no sound. Penniston touched it. The surface felt as smooth as glass and was warm to the touch. Etched along one 3-foot-wide (1 m) portion were several strange symbols. Penniston quickly sketched them in his notebook. Then came a blinding flash.

An artist's rendering of the UFO in Rendlesham Forest

Penniston and Burroughs took cover but continued to watch the ship. According to Penniston, the craft lifted up and then rapidly moved back and over the trees. "I've never seen any craft move that fast in my entire Air Force career," he said, "and I don't think I ever will again."

It seemed as though only minutes had passed, but it was now five o'clock. More than two hours had passed since Burroughs first saw the strange glow. Penniston met with a shift commander for a briefing later that morning. After hearing his story, the commander warned, "Sometimes things are best left alone." But soldiers on base were already talking about what had happened.

By the following evening, Lieutenant Colonel Charles Halt had had enough of the talk. "It was time to put this to rest," he said. He gathered a three-man security team and headed back to Rendlesham Forest. The team brought along powerful spotlights called light-alls, Geiger counters (devices used to measure radiation), cameras, and Halt's personal cassette recorder.

The soldiers couldn't get the spotlights to work. Then static overtook their walkie-talkies, as it had the night before. Halt noticed gashes in the bark of several trees and ordered members of his team to take pictures.

A Geiger counter registered readings but only on one side of a stand of trees—the side that would have faced the mysterious aircraft. As the men recorded the odd readings, something changed.

"The woods were suddenly filled with sound," Halt remembered. Barnyard animals on a nearby farm were suddenly disturbed and active. The mysterious lights had returned. What happened next was all recorded on tape.

"There it is again," one voice registered.

"I see it too," Halt responded. "What is it?"

"Don't know, sir."

"Weird," Halt murmured. "It's coming this way."

Halt and others on the team described a zigzag approach, with what appeared to be molten metal dripping from the craft as it hovered until it "silently exploded and broke into multiple white objects." The team searched the forest floor for samples of the falling metal but found nothing.

"A steady, constant beam," of light shot from the craft to the forest floor. Then the object went dark and sped away. Astonished, Halt and his team headed back to the base.

Was it all just a hoax? In 2003 Kevin Conde, a former security guard, told British reporters he'd pranked U.S. troops stationed at the RAF Bentwaters and Woodbridge bases in 1980. He said he'd parked his patrol car in an isolated part of Rendlesham Forest. He then turned his emergency lights on to make them think they'd seen something mysterious.

"It was not a UFO," he said. "It was a 1979 Plymouth Volare."

But Burroughs, Penniston, and Halt don't believe Conde's story explains what they experienced in the forest.

CRASH: NEEDLES, CALIFORNIA—2008

One of this incident's key witnesses, nicknamed Bob on the River, was always known as an unusual character in the Needles, California, area. "Everyone that knows me, knows I'm crazy," he said. But when he saw a fiery turquoise cylinder-shaped object crash just west of the Colorado River on May 14, 2008, his quiet life became a lot more public.

Las Vegas, Nevada, television reporter George Knapp covered the story. He interviewed Bob along with several other key witnesses.

"[The object] was just bright, bright enough that it illuminated the ground," said Frank Costigan, former head of security for Los Angeles International Airport. "It went behind the hill and I waited to see if I could hear it crash because as big as it was, it was bound to make a noise." But the noise never came.

Bob agreed there was no crash when he spoke to David Hayes on talk radio KTOX. He said the thing landed with a thump. Fearing a plane had gone down, Bob tried to call 911, but he couldn't get cell phone reception.

In less than twenty minutes, five government helicopters descended on the crash site. One was a Sky Crane, a helicopter designed for transporting large objects. According to Bob, the crane picked up the glowing object and headed toward Las Vegas.

George Knapp reported that several Janet planes had landed at the nearby Laughlin/Bullhead International Airport just hours before the mysterious crash. These are secret airplanes that transport employees of the Area 51 military base in southern Nevada. Dozens of "men in black" (top secret investigator) trucks and SUVs also swarmed the area the day after the event.

Knapp followed one group of the vehicles and got it to pull over. Although the men were dressed in casual civilian clothes, not suits or uniforms, they flashed government IDs and said they were federal agents with the National Nuclear Security Administration (NNSA). Knapp learned that the vehicles were from the Office of Secure Transportation (OST). The OST is responsible for transporting top secret cargo across the United States.

Was this UFO extraterrestrial? Author Kevin D. Randle says that's unlikely. Someone was carefully tracking the object, so someone knew what it was—a reminder that not all UFOs originate in outer space. Some may be American made.

A Sky Crane similar to this one picked up a mysterious glowing object that landed near Needles, California, in 2008.

IMAGINE... Yllek is not alone on this strange planet. He walks slowly toward the mysterious creature. "Is it dangerous?" he asks himself. "Does it mean me any harm?" He wonders if the creature is as frightened as he is. He can't read the thoughts of this creature the way he can with his own kind. But as the creature's expression seems to warm, Yllek feels at ease.

CHAPTER THREE:
THE ALIENS

Many reports of UFOs have been recorded. We even have convincing tales of landings and crashes. But the question remains: who is piloting those UFOs? Some experts suggest the UFOs may be unoccupied probes sent to investigate planet Earth. This is similar to the unmanned probes we have sent to Mars. Others say aliens control the UFOs but rarely interact with unsuspecting humans. Is this possible? For centuries, religious leaders considered it a crime to even suggest it. But opinions have shifted.

In May 2008, Father Jose Gabriel Funes, Catholic director of the Vatican Observatory near Rome, Italy, said, "Just as there is a multiplicity of creatures over the earth, so there could be other beings, even intelligent [beings], created by God."

Hundreds of people worldwide tell stories of face-to-face encounters with those "other beings." Are they representatives from alien worlds? If these stories are true, the answer may be yes.

This illustration shows what might have happened after the 1947 UFO crash in Roswell, New Mexico.

Roswell Revisited—1947

We've explored the 1947 UFO crash in Roswell, New Mexico. But some witnesses say more than UFOs fell to Earth on that stormy summer night. They believe alien bodies were scattered along with the mysterious debris.

Missouri State University janitor Gerald Anderson was a small child in 1947, but his memories are clear. "I remember huge black eyes," he told the *MSU Standard* newspaper. "You could see their muscles move. They were not human, and I'll maintain that until the day I die. God only knows where they were from or how far they were from home. Their toy was broke and their situation seemed impossible."

According to the *Standard* article, Anderson believes two ships went down on the night of July 3, 1947. He theorizes that one ship was struck by lightning, which sent it crashing into the other. After the collision, both ships went down—one in Corona, New Mexico, and the other along the plains of San Agustin, New Mexico. Anderson says that he and his family were hiking in the San Agustin plains when they came across a UFO and four aliens. Not long after, the military arrived. They did not seem surprised about the ship or the aliens.

Anderson recognizes that some people may not believe what he saw. "[The military knew] what was there," he said. "Until a piece of physical evidence is found, nobody's going to believe this."

Giovanni Schiaparelli and H. G. Wells

Did grey aliens enter the public imagination in 1947? Perhaps, but British author H. G. Wells—famous for writing the alien classic *War of the Worlds*—described something similar in 1893.

In 1877 Italian astronomer Giovanni Schiaparelli saw through a telescope what he called *canali* on the surface of Mars. The word *canali* can mean channels, or canals, in Italian. In scientific reports, Schiaparelli wondered if ancient life on Mars might have created canali before it went extinct.

People were amazed. Could intelligent life have existed on Mars? And what would it mean if it had? H. G. Wells also wondered about extraterrestrial life. But what really captured his imagination was the possibility of humankind heading toward extinction on Earth. He wrote about such changes in his essay, "The Man of the Year Million."

Sixteen years after Schiaparelli's reports, Wells predicted the power of the intellect would eventually make the body unnecessary. In an essay, he described people with huge, "bulbous" heads to house their swollen brains. Their skin was pale from lack of sunlight, and bodies were fragile because of lack of exercise.

"Great hands they have, enormous brains, soft, liquid, soulful eyes," he wrote. "Their whole muscular system, their legs, their abdomens, are shriveled to nothing, a dangling degraded pendant to their minds."

Could the witnesses who described grey aliens have been influenced by Wells's fiction? Could Wells have had close encounters of his own? It's hard to say. But reports of close encounters with greys continue—and so does the search for proof.

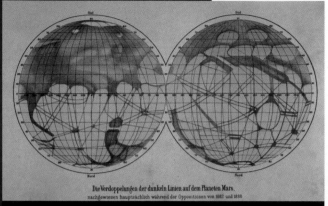

Die Verdoppelungen der dunkeln Linien auf dem Planeten Mars,
nachgewiesen hauptsächlich während der Oppositionen von 1882 und 1888

Giovanni Schiaparelli created this map of canals on Mars in the late 1800s.

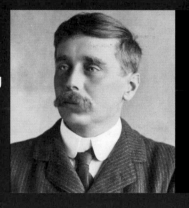

H. G. Wells in about 1908

Ruwa, Zimbabwe—1994

On the morning of September 16, 1994, the children at Arial School in Ruwa, Zimbabwe, were playing outside. The adults were indoors preparing for the rest of the hot school day. It was 91°F (33°C) in the shade. The children's screams and squeals reached a new high, but no one thought a thing of it. After all, kids are always loud at recess, aren't they?

But the sixty-two children between the ages of six and twelve poured back into class with an amazing story. According to the young witnesses, three silver balls appeared in the sky over the school. They disappeared with a flash and then reappeared several times in other locations. When they finally settled in a thorny area about 328 feet (100 m) from the playground, a small being about 3 feet (1 m) tall appeared at the top of the largest ball. He descended to the sharp, rough ground before noticing the crowd of children and then disappeared.

The small man, or one just like him, reappeared. One eleven-year-old witness described him as being scrawny with a big head and large, dark eyes. She said his skin was pale and he had long dark hair that fell below his shoulders.

"They were just looking at us," said one of the older girls when she was interviewed for a documentary. "They were like kind of astonished at what we were. I got scared because I've never seen a person like that before."

A younger girl agreed, saying, "The face, just the eyes, they looked horrible."

When the children were encouraged to create drawings of what they'd seen, they drew very similar images of the alien life-form. A young student thought the visitor wanted to eat her. Her fear was probably influenced by the local legends about *tokoloshes*, or bogeymen, which are supposed to eat children. The older witnesses had a different perspective.

A drawing by one of the young children who saw the strange creature in Ruwa, Zimbabwe, in 1994

"I think they want people to know that we're actually making harm on this world," said one student. "We mustn't get too technological."

Harvard medical school psychiatrist John Mack interviewed more than a dozen of the kids. In his career, he had spoken with many people who claimed to have encounters with aliens. He concluded, "This seems to be what it is. It seems to have no other psychiatric explanation."

One final witness agreed. "I haven't been influenced by any of my friends," she said. "I've simply seen what I've seen."

Huay Nam Rak, Thailand—2005

On the morning of Friday, September 9, 2005, more than ten residents of Huay Nam Rak, Thailand, saw what they described as an extraterrestrial being. They were in a rice field.

"The alien is about 70 cm [2.3 feet] high and has yellow skin and [a] flat chest," said witness Sawaeng Boonyalak in the *Nation* newspaper. "Its mouth is very tiny. It has [a] bald, big head with big eyes and big ears." He went on to say the visitor wandered around the field for more than an hour with no concern for who could see it.

"Suddenly, the alien floated to a tree top," he continued. "After more villagers came to see it, it floated into the sky into the bright light." Buakaew Intaweng at first thought the alien was an inflated children's toy but saw it move from place to place and changed her mind.

Media and government analysts don't agree on the report's authenticity. Some say it was a case of mistaken identity. Others say reports from so many witnesses could reflect a real alien sighting. For now, the truth is uncertain.

Workers in a rice field in northern Thailand

Monahans, Texas—2009

Something unusual happened when one anonymous family from near Monahans, Texas, gathered on December 11, 2009, for a birthday celebration. According to an eyewitness report filed with MUFON (case 20985), a family representative said, "Two of my nephews and a niece came tearing into the house, screaming at the top of their lungs, saying a plane had crashed in one of the adjacent pastures."

The smell of burning mesquite (a thorny tree common to the area) filled the air, but it didn't worry the adults as they walked outside to investigate. "It was nippy," the witness said. "Someone could have been burning wood in their [fireplace]."

"As we cleared a stand of trees," the witness said, "we were shocked to see an oval shaped object hovering, maybe 4 to 5 feet [1.2 to 1.5 m] off the ground."

Light from distant streetlights seemed to bounce off the polished silver metal of the strange aircraft. The craft was nearly 30 feet (9 m) long and almost as wide. It emitted a soft, blue light. "I can only imagine that our jaws were probably on the ground," the witness said.

Two strange, humanlike life-forms walked around from the back of the hovering craft. They were gathering objects from the trees and the ground. "They looked very skinny," the witness reported, "like they had no meat on their bones. Their heads were large and their arms . . . hung down around their knees."

The busy visitors didn't notice the Texas family at first. But when the two nephews joined them in the clearing and one cried out, "What are those things?" the aliens were alerted.

The visitors did not threaten the family. They simply looked at them for a few seconds with large eyes, "like the eyes of a praying mantis," the witnesses said. Then they walked to the rear of the ship and disappeared.

Seconds later, the craft rose silently. "No rush of wind, not even a swaying of the nearby mesquite trees," the witness said. It hovered about 40 feet (12 m) from the ground and then shot straight up into the air, glowing as it faded out of sight.

"I never really believed in UFOs or aliens," the witness said at the end of the report. "But after the events of this night, I'm seriously going to reevaluate that belief."

Some experiences are hard—if not impossible—to deny, though one local Monahans newspaper said the report was proven to be false.

Witnesses described seeing an alien similar to this one in Monahans, Texas.

Greys

Reptilians

Nordics

Greys

Greys are the alien life-forms described by most witnesses. According to some experts, greys appear in up to 75 percent of credible reports. They are said to have the following physical characteristics:

- Bipedal—standing upright on two legs
- Short—between 3 and 4 feet (1 and 1.2 m) tall
- Slight—only about 40 pounds (18 kilograms)
- Oversized head—larger than human heads
- Earless—no ears or no visible ears
- No nose—or only slits where nostrils might be

- Large eyes—two big, dark colored, almond-shaped eyes
- No mouth—or just a slit where a mouth might be
- Smooth-skinned—hairless, silver, tan, or pale blue bodies
- Long arms—graceful, long arms with thin, four-fingered hands
- Slight legs—thin, short legs

Greys are also called Zetas, or Roswell aliens. Some people believe greys were never reported before 1947.

Reptilians

While most reports of alien encounters involve greys, some witnesses describe what's known as a reptilian, or reptoid. This is the second most common alien type. It is said to exhibit these characteristics:

- Bipedal—standing upright on two legs
- Tall—between 5 and 7 feet (1.5 and 2 m) tall
- Slim—lean but muscular build
- Proportional limbs—arms and legs similar in length to human arms and legs

- Scaly skin similar to traditional reptile species
- Clawed hands like traditional reptile species
- Large eyes—gold or green, similar to reptiles

Comic books and television programs have featured reptilian aliens for years. But in 1895, long before modern comic books existed, novelist Edgar Fawcett included them in his work. Before Fawcett, Native American legends (including Hopi and Mayan) told of reptilian gods and demons.

Nordics

Witnesses sometimes describe other alien types including insectoid (insectlike creatures) and oranges (humanoid creatures with orange hair and skin). But the third most common alien is called a Nordic, or humanoid.

These aliens look very much like humans but also have alien characteristics. Their eyes allegedly have an **inner lid**, like some known reptiles, to help filter out ultraviolet light. And they supposedly have fewer teeth. Apart from those subtle differences, Nordics are reportedly identical to Earthlings in every way.

inner lid

Dale Russell and Dinosaurian Evolution

Dale Russell is NOT an alien expert. He's a scientist and former curator of paleontology at the North Carolina Museum of Natural Sciences. In 1982 one of his ideas about dinosaurs crossed into the realm of the reptoid alien.

Dinosaurs went extinct 65 million years ago. But in 1982, Russell proposed a new possibility. What if *Troodon*, one of the smartest dinosaurs ever to walk on Earth, had escaped extinction and continued to evolve? What if it had become what Russell calls a dinosauroid?

Not once did the scientist say this scenario DID unfold. It was pure fiction. But Russell did allow himself to imagine what *Troodon* could have become. In his imagination, the dinosaur's brain grew bigger and more capable of complex thought. To make up for the extra weight, the dinosaur's posture changed. It began to carry his head higher, above its hips instead of ahead of them.

Troodon's physical needs changed too. It no longer needed a long tail to balance out its forward-leaning head. So slowly, the tail grew smaller or disappeared completely. Its eyes grew larger and closer together. Its torso grew more muscular, and its arms and legs grew more humanlike in proportion. Claws still grew at the ends of its longer fingers, but they were more flexible.

With help from artist Ron Seguin, Russell created a lifelike sculpture of his evolved dinosaur. According to author Brad Steiger, who studies eyewitness reports of encounters with aliens, dozens of people who believe they've seen reptilian aliens see something familiar in Russell's sculpture. Could life on other planets have gone reptilian?

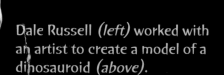

Dale Russell *(left)* worked with an artist to create a model of a dinosauroid *(above)*.

IMAGINE… their amazement. Yllek offers the boy a tour of the shuttle. The boy accepts. He shares everything he has in his pockets and even a lock of his hair. The crew marvels at his belongings, amused by the images in his book. Yllek offers the boy items in trade—rocks and trinkets from his home planet.

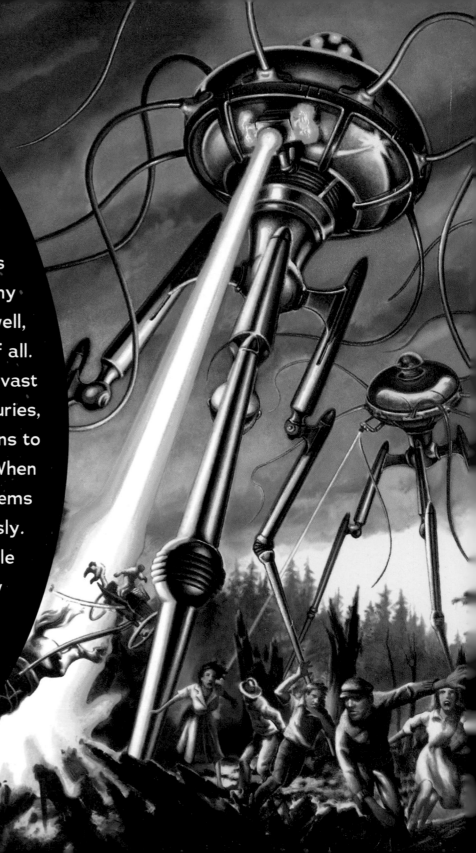

CHAPTER FOUR:
HOAXES AND MISUNDERSTANDINGS

Some people think all UFO and alien sightings are hoaxes—events staged to fool people on purpose. Many skeptics list the 1947 crash at Roswell, New Mexico, as the biggest hoax of all. Others firmly disagree. Why the vast difference of opinions? For centuries, people have searched for explanations to the mysteries of our natural world. When science can answer a question, it seems reasonable to take the answer seriously. When science cannot, things get a little cloudy. UFOs and aliens fall in a cloudy space. Without proof—one way or the other—people will continue to disagree. Even if UFOs and aliens are real, that doesn't mean that everything having to do with them is real. Here are some of the best-known hoaxes and misunderstandings.

War of the Worlds—1938

Novelist H. G. Wells wrote *The War of the Worlds*—a story of Martians invading London, England, in 1898. It was one of the first fictional tales to pit human beings against alien visitors.

Forty years later—in 1938—actor Orson Welles (*photo below*) created a radio production, adapting the British novel for U.S. listeners. On the night before Halloween, almost two million listeners all over the country heard an actor portraying a newsman tell the story of mysterious objects crashing in New Jersey, followed by a more startling claim. Martians had attacked.

"I knew it was a hoax," said Henry Brylawski in a 2005 interview. But he admitted his girlfriend's sister was terrified. "She thought the news was real," he said. She was not alone.

Thousands of listeners flooded their local police departments with panicked calls, making it one of the most famous UFO misunderstandings ever reported. Why were people so easy to fool? Most tuned into the show late and missed the performance's introduction, explaining it was a fictional drama. World events also had an effect. German dictator Adolf Hitler had recently begun invading other European countries. Did he pose a threat to the United States as well? The fear of a foreign attack was very real. Wells regretted the misunderstanding but was confused by how listeners reacted. Before the performance, he had been concerned the story was too unbelievable for people to enjoy. The exact opposite occurred.

Kevin D. Randle has advanced degrees in both psychology and the art of military science. He has served as an army helicopter pilot, intelligence officer, and military police officer and in the U.S. Air Force as an intelligence and public affairs officer. He did tours of duty during the Vietnam War (1959-1975) and in the recent war in Iraq (2003-present). He retired from active duty in 2009 as a lieutenant colonel in the Iowa National Guard.

Randle uses his extensive investigative experience to help research and write about aliens and UFOs. He has published more than eighty books.

Are there any signs in the early steps of UFO research that let you know something might be a hoax?

Usually, early on, there isn't anything to suggest [a] hoax or that something real was observed. You have to listen to what the people say, see if it makes sense, watch their body language to see if there are any clues there, and then follow up with corroboration. One of the big clues is when the witness says, "I don't care what the facts are" or "I don't care what anyone thinks" or "I don't have to prove anything." That sort of language and attitude suggests that there is no evidence or proof. Those who have it are always willing to provide it. Those who don't have it offer excuses.

What is the most frequent explanation for the average UFO sighting that is not a UFO?

Venus is probably mistaken for a UFO more often than anything else. Most people don't realize just how bright Venus can be and that the atmosphere provides effects that suggest spotlights or engines.

For UFO crashes, I think bolides, which are very bright meteors, might be the thing most often mistaken for UFOs, especially as they break up. People don't realize that they can appear to be a single craft with lighted windows and that they are often accompanied by a roaring sound.

In your research, have you ever noticed any one kind of UFO is sighted more often than another?

That has changed over the years. I think a disk was seen more often in the early years, but now we seem to get a lot of triangular-shaped objects. This is just my impression and not based on any sort of statistical study.

Which three UFO sightings do you consider the most credible?

Roswell; the 1957 Levelland, Texas, sightings; and the Bendwaters/Rendlesham Forest sightings in the United Kingdom.

What advice do you have for kids who would like to study the skies in search of UFOs?

Know what is in the sky and what it looks like. Study the star charts and learn about comets and meteors. Learn about the auto kinesis, which are the small movements of the eye that make a pinpoint of light (such as a star) seem to move around in a random pattern. Learn what others thought were UFOs and what the solutions for those sightings were.

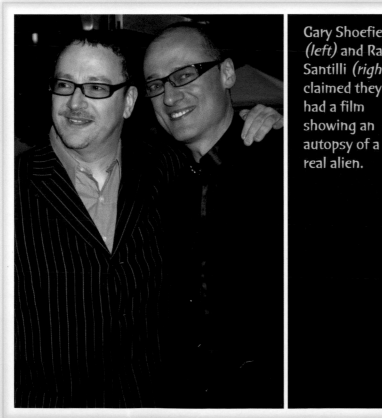

Gary Shoefield *(left)* and Ray Santilli *(right)* claimed they had a film showing an autopsy of a real alien.

Alien Autopsy—1995

Roswell's 1947 crash had credible witnesses that insisted the UFO was real. But that doesn't mean everything associated with the crash was real. In 1995 British businessmen Ray Santilli and Gary Shoefield released what they called authentic film footage of an alien body autopsy. It featured doctors and nurses trying to save a wounded grey alien and later performing an autopsy. Santilli and Shoefield said it was filmed at the crash site in New Mexico. Millions of people watched their documentary with a mix of awe and skepticism. Skepticism was the more appropriate reaction.

Sculptor and special effects artist John Humphreys admitted in 2006 that he had created the alien model featured in the documentary. Santilli and Shoefield claim they had actual film footage from 1947 but that it was badly damaged. "[The film] was disintegrating," Humphreys said, "so they asked me if I could interpret what I could see and help them to restore it. In effect, it was a documentary. But what you see in the original 1995 film, the alien is what I made."

Real or hoax, Humphreys is confident his alien is as close to real as a replica can get. "A billion people, worldwide, have seen the alien autopsy film footage, and I have had many compliments e-mailed to me," he said in a 2007 interview. "I would like to create a 'living' version," he admitted. Using animatronics, the model would seem even more lifelike.

The creature he did create required months of artistic effort. "The sculpture was made first in clay," he said, "and it took a month with minor adjustments." Once the sculpture was complete, a more durable model had to be crafted. "It was molded in fiberglass and cast into latex, then painted," said Humphreys.

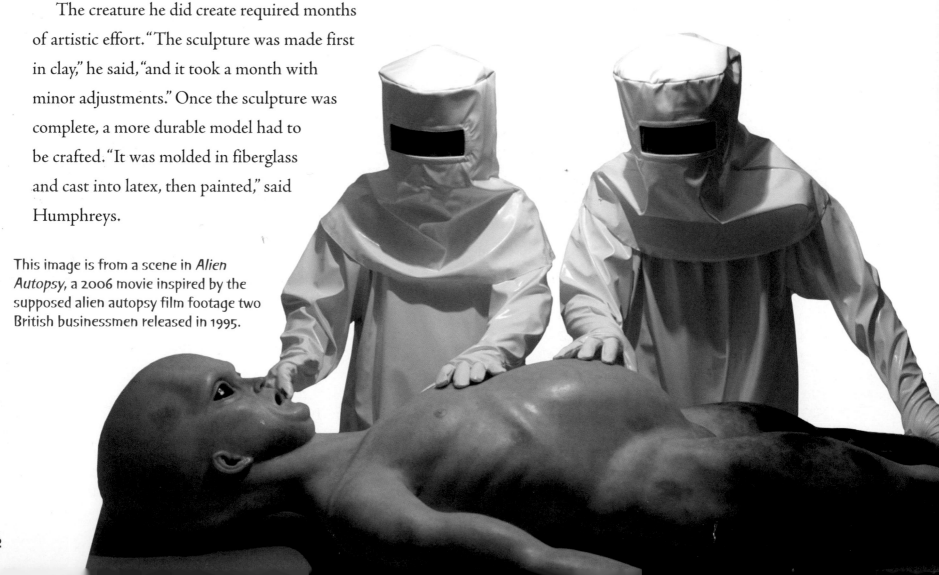

This image is from a scene in *Alien Autopsy*, a 2006 movie inspired by the supposed alien autopsy film footage two British businessmen released in 1995.

When screenwriter Barney Broom was renovating his family home in 2006, he made an unexpected find. Stashed in the attic, wrapped in a 1947 newspaper was a jar with what appeared to be a tiny baby alien floating inside. Could it be real? Considering the newspaper was published the same year as the U.S. Roswell incident, Broom couldn't help but wonder.

Thorough investigation proved the captive alien was either a hoax or an art piece. It was a sculpture made of clay. But the question remained. Who created the strange baby alien and why? Bloom shared his thoughts.

Can you tell us about how you discovered the alien in the jar?

I discovered the alien in the jar while renovating my house. Because the property is about 20 miles [32 km] from Mildenhall, a major U.S. Air Force base [where UFOs have allegedly been documented], people wondered if it had anything to do with the Roswell incident and Wright-Patterson air base in America.

What was your first reaction to the discovery?

Nonplussed [confused] is the answer. If it was a trick, it was well done. The paper in which the jar was wrapped was a 1947 *Daily Mirror*. The jar was obviously from the same period, and the "alien" was perfectly formed inside it.

It could be a hoax, but judging from all the dust and other debris in the loft, and the fact that no one had lived in the house for a couple of years prior to my purchasing the place, it must have been done quite some time ago.

What did the newspaper say?

You may find this odd, but I was so struck by the alien, I didn't read the papers. I only noted that it was dated 1947. I do know the genuineness of the paper was authenticated.

What was the strangest thing about finding the alien?

People's acceptance of it. Some of the radio interviews I gave involved people who weren't cranks [crazy people]. They were quite well known in UK public life— people you'd think, "Hey, there must be something to it if he/she is speaking about it seriously."

This photo of Barney Broom with the alien in a jar he found in his attic was first published by the *Guardian* newspaper in the United Kingdom.

CONCLUSION: REAL OR UNREAL?

Seth Shostak is the senior astronomer for the Search for Extraterrestrial Intelligence Institute (SETI). SETI's mission is to explore, understand, and explain the origin, nature, and prevalence—or frequency—of life in the universe. Shostak does not believe UFOs are piloted by beings from distant planets. He believes most can be explained. But at a SETI conference in August 2010, he predicted that within twenty-five years, proof of intelligent extraterrestrial life would be found.

Planetary astronomer and researcher Wang Sichao has a differing opinion. After years of study at the Purple Hills Observatory of the Chinese Academy of Science, he stated in August 2010 that extraterrestrial beings do exist and have the ability to visit Earth. He urged scientists to design better telescopes to track and photograph the agile, speedy ships.

Without undeniable proof—an extraterrestrial spacecraft and alien flight crew openly studied by a team of international scientists and revealed to the public—the debate will doubtless continue. For now, we can only piece together probable answers based on eyewitness reports, reasonable theories, questions, and possible scientific answers.

For example, are all UFOs spaceships from other planets? According to MUFON, the answer is no. Most UFO sightings are actually tricks of the eye—stars, meteors, planets, and even little-known weather events mistaken for UFOs. Some may even be sophisticated man-made aircraft, or top secret planes, almost as hard to prove as alien spacecraft. But many governments are beginning to take the topic seriously.

In March 2007, the Centre National d'Etudes Spatiales (CNES) released 6,000 official UFO reports from the French government's secret files. After careful analysis by government investigators, most of the observations had been debunked. But 14 percent, or 840, of the reports could not be explained.

Just over a year later, in May 2008, the British government released more than 150 UFO files compiled by the Ministry of Defense (MoD) between 1978 and 2002. UFO researcher and twenty-one-year MoD veteran Nick Pope said in a *Telegraph* newspaper article, "Most of the UFO sightings here are probably misidentifications of aircraft lights and meteors, but some are more difficult to explain."

This flying saucer is actually a V2-9 Avrocar, an experimental aircraft developed for the U.S. Air Force in the 1950s.

In August 2010, Brazil announced it would require that all reports, including photographs, of UFO sightings be carefully documented and then released to the public.

The U.S. government has not been as open. For decades it has denied keeping UFO files. But information released in November 2005 told another story. According to the Federation of American Scientists, 239 secret UFO reports are on file at the National Security Agency— most filed between 1958 and 1979.

While the actual files have not been released, some of the file titles, including "UFO Hypothesis and Survival Questions," and

This 1984 photo may show a UFO over São Paulo, Brazil.

"UFO's and the Intelligence Community Blind Spot to Surprise or Deceptive Data" have been revealed. These are interesting headings for a nation that denies that UFOs exist.

Other UFO-related documents have been filed under misleading titles. Documentary producer John Greenewald Jr. has spent more than fifteen years trying to find and explore those documents. He makes written requests through the U.S. Freedom of Information Act (FOIA), collects them by the thousands, and posts them online. But some remain out of his reach.

According to Greenewald, UFO files considered a threat to national security are archived at the North American Aerospace Defense Command (NORAD). These files are blocked from all FOIA requests.

For now UFO research in the United States is a little like a game of hide-and-seek. So researchers depend on what documents they can find along with the statements of trustworthy eyewitnesses to build a case that UFO are real. What have people seen? How can those sightings be explained? Keep searching for new information and decide for yourself.

IMAGINE... as Yllek pilots his shuttle toward the mother ship, his crew members document the evidence collected from the earthling. He is overwhelmed at what he's experienced. As the shuttle nears the mother ship, something strange appears in the distance. "We are not alone," Yllek says with a smile. "This is only the beginning."

Mineral, Washington

Levelland,
Texas

Kecksburg, Pennsylvania

Needles, California

Washington, D.C.

Phoenix, Arizona

Roswell, New Mexico

FLORIDA EVERGLADES

Monahans, Texas

NORTH
AMERICA

SOUTH
AMERICA

UFO sighting

UFO landing/crash

Alien sighting

Incidents Featured in This Book

UNITED KINGDOM

RAF BENTWATERS

RENDLESHAM FOREST

RAF WOODBRIDGE

RENDLESHAM FOREST, UK

EUROPE

ASIA

Tehran, Iran

Hangzhou, China

Huay Nam Rak, Thailand

AFRICA

Ruwa, Zimbabwe

AUSTRALIA

GLOSSARY

aerospace: an industry that deals with travel in and above Earth's atmosphere. It also deals with making vehicles used in this travel.

agile: ability to move easily and quickly

allegedly: describes an unproven claim

animatronics: a puppet or other figure that can move because of electrical devices inside

bipedal: standing on two feet

corroboration: support from additional evidence or witnesses

debunk: expose as false

discount: to believe certain information is not important or correct

emit: to release, or send out, light, sound, or heat

evasive: action to make escape possible

extraterrestrial: existing beyond Earth

hoax: an act meant to trick or deceive people

inhabit: to live in or on

light-year: the distance light travels in one year. One light-year is equal to 6 trillion miles (9.5 trillion km).

molten: melted

mother ship: large craft or home base to a fleet of smaller craft

ovoid: egg-shaped

propulsion: the force that moves something forward

rash: a series of similar events taking place over a short period of time

rational: reasonable and logical

retract: to say an earlier statement is not true

scramble: to quickly send up one or more planes

self-inflicted: done to oneself

skepticism: an attitude of doubt

slight: slim, delicate build

tailed: followed

transistor: a small device that controls the flow of electricity in objects such as radios and computers

UFO: unidentified flying object

SOURCE NOTES

8–9   Stanton Friedman, interview with the author, August 16, 2010.

14   Robert Sheaffer, "The Truth Is, They Never Were 'Saucers,'" Committee for Skeptical Inquiry, October 1997, http://www.csicop.org/si/show/truth_is_they_never_were_saucers/ (October 4, 2011).

14   Richard Hall, "The 1952 Sighting Wave," NICAP.org, August 27, 2011, http://www.nicap.org/waves/1952fullrep.htm (October 4, 2011).

15   Jerome Clark, *The UFO Book: Encyclopedia of the Extraterrestrial* (Detroit: Visible Ink Press, 1998), 654.

15   Ronald D. Story, ed., *The Encyclopedia of Extraterrestrial Encounters: A Definitive Illustrated A-Z Guide to All Things Alien* (New York: New American Library, 2001), 844–845.

15   Cherlyn Gardner Strong, "This Day in Paranormal History: 'Washington Flap' UFO Wave of 1952," July 27, 2010, *Tucson Citizen*, http://tucsoncitizen.com/paranormal/2010/07/27/this-day-in-paranormal-history-washington-flap-ufo-wave-of-1952/ (October 3, 2011).

16–17   "Case Summary: Everglades, Florida, 1965," *UFO Evidence*, n.d., http://www.ufoevidence.org/cases/case165.htm (October 3, 2011).

18   Belinda Perdew Taylor, interview with the author, August 2, 2010.

20   Lynne D. Kitei, *The Phoenix Lights* (Charlottesville, MA: Hampton Roads Publishing, 2004), 4.

21   *Xpose UFO Truth*, "It Was a Boomerang/Diamond Shape with Lights at Each Point," March 26, 1997, http://fierycelt.tripod.com/xposeufotruth/1990s02.html (October 3, 2011).

22   Associated Press, "Former Arizona Governor Boosts UFO Claims," *MSNBC*, March 23, 2007, http://www.msnbc.msn.com/id/17761943/ns/technology_and_science-space/t/former-ariz-governor-boosts-ufo-claims/#.Tki8L2FvCgA (October 3, 2011).

22   Casey Bayer, "UFO Over Chinese Airport," *Christian Science Monitor*, July 16, 2010, http://www.csmonitor.com/Science/Discoveries/2010/0716/UFO-over-Chinese-airport-VIDEO (October 3, 2011).

23   *Daily Mail* reporter, "Chinese Airport Closed after Fiery UFO is Spotted Flying over City," *Daily Mail*, July 16, 2010, http://www.dailymail.co.uk/sciencetech/article-1293395/UFO-China-closes-Xiaoshan-Airport-spotted-flying-city.html (October 5, 2011).

23   *Tucson Citizen*, "Team of Experts in China Release 'China UFO' Findings," July 26, 2010, http://tucsoncitizen.com/paranormal/tag/xiaoshan-airport/page/2/ (October 3, 2011).

24   Michael Schratt, interview with the author, July 31, 2010.

28   Charles Berlitz, *The Roswell Incident* (New York: Grosset and Dunlap, 1980), 28.

28   *Roswell Daily Record*, "RAAF Captures Flying Saucer on Ranch in Roswell Region," July 8, 1947, 1.

29   Jesse Marcel Jr., interview with the author, June 17, 2010.

30   *Washington Evening Star*, "Fiery Object Reported in Wide Area Over Texas," November 4, 1957, A-5.

31   Story, *The Encyclopedia of Extraterrestrial Encounters*, 306–308.

32   Kevin D. Randle, *Crash: When UFOs Fall from the Sky: A History of Famous Incidents, Conspiracies, and Cover-ups* (Franklin Lakes, NJ: New Page Books, 2010), 208.

32   Ibid., 210.

33   James Penniston, in *UFO Files*, episode no. 14, first broadcast December 17, 2005, by the History Channel, produced by David Digangi and written by David Digangi.

34   Ibid.

34   Ibid.

34   Ibid.

34   Ibid.

35   Ibid.

35   Ibid.

35   Ibid.

35   BBC, "Rendlesham UFO Hoax," *BBC Inside Out,* June 30, 2003, http://www.bbc.co.uk/insideout/east/series3/rendlesham_ufos. shtml (October 3, 2011).

35   Bob on the River, interviewed by George Knapp, *I-Team,* KLAS-TV, Las Vegas, November 1, 2008.

36   Frank Costigan, interviewed by George Knapp, *I-Team,* KLAS-TV, Las Vegas, July 31, 2008.

39   CNA, "Believing in Aliens Not Opposed to Christianity, Vatican's Top Astronomer Says," *Catholic News Agency,* May 13, 2008, http://www.catholicnewsagency.com/news/believing_in_aliens_not_opposed_to_christianity_vaticans_top_astronomer_says/ (October 3, 2011).

39   Becky Long, "Alien Witness, Former Navy SEAL Shares Colorful Past with Students," *Missouri State University Standard,* February 28, 2001, http://www.the-standard.org/news/alien-witness-former-navy-seal-shares-colorful-past-with-students/article_92787e7c-6bf1-5b0c-a054-3c05fec0f2a6.html (October 5, 2011).

39   Ibid.

40   David Szondy, "1,000,000 AD," *Tales of Future Past,* n.d., http://davidszondy.com/future/man/man_million.htm, (October 3, 2011).

41   Cynthia Hind, "1994 Close Encounter at Ruwa Zimbabwe," *UFO Casebook,* n.d., http://www.ufocasebook.com/2008b/1994zimbabwe.html (October 3, 2011).

41   Ibid.

41   Ibid.

41   Ibid.

41   Ibid.

42   "Villagers in Thailand Witness Two-Foot Tall 'Alien' Being in Rice Field," *UFO Evidence,* September 9, 2005, http://www.ufoevidence .org/cases/case490.htm (October 3, 2011).

42   Ibid.

42   "Strange Encounter in Texas—MUFON Report," *Bugg's Blog,* December 11, 2009, http://ptbuggy.wordpress.com/2009/12/14/strange-encounter-in-texas-mufon-report/ (October 3, 2011).

49   Stefan Lovgen, "'War of the Worlds': Behind the 1938 Radio Show Panic," *National Geographic News,* June 17, 2005, http://news .nationalgeographic.com/news/2005/06/0617_050617_warworlds .html (October 3, 2011).

50   Kevin Randle, interview with the author, August 14, 2010.

52   John Humphreys, interview with the author, October 28, 2007, November 4, 2007, and November 10, 2007.

52   Ibid.

52   Ibid.

53   Barney Broom, interview with the author, October 30, 2007.

55   Matthew McCreary, "Are There Ulster Sightings in Whitehall's UFO Files?," *Belfast Telegraph,* May 16, 2008, http://www.telegraph .co.uk/news/uknews/1952867/British-Government-releases-UFO-files.html (October 3, 2011).

SELECTED BIBLIOGRAPHY

Berliner, Don, and Stanton T. Friedman. *Crash at Corona.* New York: Paraview Special Editions, 2004.

Birnes, William J. *The UFO Magazine UFO Encyclopedia.* New York: Pocket Books, 2004.

Friedman, Stanton T. *Flying Saucers and Science: A Scientist Investigates the Mysteries of UFOs.* Franklin Lakes, NJ: New Page Books, 2008.

Kean, Leslie. *UFOs: Generals, Pilots, and Government Officials Go on the Record.* New York: Harmony Books, 2010

Kitei, Lynne D. *The Phoenix Lights.* Charlottesville, VA: Hampton Roads Publishing, 2004.

Marcel, Jesse, Jr. *The Roswell Legacy: The Untold Story of the First Military Officer at the 1947 Crash Site.* Franklin Lakes, NJ: Career Press, 2009.

Mutual UFO Network. http://www.mufon.com/.

National UFO Reporting Center. http://www.nwlink.com/~ufocntr/.

Randle, Kevin D. *Crash: When UFOs Fall from the Sky: A History of Famous Incidents, Conspiracies, and Cover-ups.* Franklin Lakes, NJ: New Page Books, 2010.

Story, Ronald D., ed. *The Encyclopedia of Extraterrestrial Encounters: A Definitive Illustrated A-Z Guide to All Things Alien.* New York: New American Library, 2001.

UFO Digest. http://www.ufodigest.com/index.php.

UFO Evidence. http://www.ufoevidence.org/.

UFO Magazine. http://www.ufomag.com/.

UFO ORGANIZATIONS

Eager to know more about UFOs and aliens?
Check out these organizations for more information including newsletters, books, conferences, and local meetings.

Institute for Cooperation in Space
http://www.peaceinspace.com

International UFO Congress
http://ufocongress.com

Mutual UFO Network (MUFON)
http://www.mufon.com

National UFO Reporting Center
http://www.nuforc.org

SETI Institute
http://www.seti.org

UFO FESTIVALS

Bridgeville UFO Festival—California
http://www.humboldtliving.com/display.php?event=2692

Exeter UFO Festival—New Hampshire
http://exeterufofestival.com/

Fyffe UFO Days—Alabama
http://www.facebook.com/FyffeUFODays

Kecksburg UFO Festival—Pennsylvania
http://www.kecksburgvfd.com/

Roswell UFO Festival—New Mexico
http://www.roswellufofestival.com/

UFO Fest—Oregon
http://www.ufofest.com/

Ventura County UFO Festival—California
http://www.facebook.com/VenturaCountyUFOFestival

PHOTO ACKNOWLEDGMENTS

The images in this book are used with the permission of: © Dmitriy Karelin/Dreamstime.com, pp. 1, 3, 4, 6 (left), 12, 26, 38, 44, 45, 48, 54, 60, 61, 62, 63, 64 and all starry backgrounds; © Aaron Foster/Photographer's Choice/Getty Images, pp. 2-3; NASA/MSFC, p. 6 (right); NASA/JSC, pp. 6-7; © Paramount Television/The Kobal Collection/Art Resource, NY, p. 7; © iStockphoto.com/Uyen Le, pp. 8-9, 19, 24, 29, 50-51, 53; © Kelly Milner Halls, pp. 8, 50 (inset); © Fortean Picture Library, pp. 9 (both), 10, 12-13, 34, 38-39, 41, 54-55 (top), 56; © Mary Evans Picture Library/The Image Works, p. 14 (top); © David Boyer/NGS Collection/The Art Archive/Art Resource, NY, p. 15; © Andrew H. Brown/NGS Collection/The Art Archive/Art Resource, NY, p. 16 (bottom); NASA/KSC, p. 17 (top); AP Photo/Elaine Thompson, p. 18 (top); AP Photo/Phuoc, p. 18 (bottom); © Belinda Perdew Taylor, p. 19; © Tim Ley 1997, p. 20 (bottom); © Lynne D. Kitei, M.D., p. 21; U.S. Navy photo by Photographer's Mate Airman Jhi L. Scott, p. 22 (top); © Peter Parks/AFP/Getty Images, p. 23; AP Photo/Ralph Fountain, p. 24 (inset); © David Hardy/Photo Researchers, Inc., pp. 26-27; © Brian Cahn/ZUMA Press, p. 27 (left); © iStockphoto.com/Don Bayley, pp. 27 (right), 28, 30, 31, 32, 33, 34, 35, 36; © United States Air Force/AFP/Getty Images, p. 28; © Victor Habbick Visions/Photo Researchers, Inc., p. 31; © Annie O'Neill/Chicago Tribune/MCT via Getty Images, p. 32 (inset); © Ray Moreton/Keystone/Hulton Archive/Getty Images, p. 33 (top); © Jvdwolf/Dreamstime.com, p. 36; © Mary Evans Picture Library/Michael Buhler/The Image Works, p. 39; © Detlev van Ravenswaay/Photo Researchers, Inc., p. 40 (top); © Reginald Haines/Hulton Archive/Getty Images, p. 40 (bottom); © Eurasia/Robert Harding World Imagery/Getty Images, p. 42; © Dan Burn-Forti/Stone/Getty Images, p. 43; AP Photo/The News & Observer, Christobal Perez, p. 46 (left); © Jonathan Blair/CORBIS, p. 46 (right); © Joe DeVito, pp. 48-49; © Hulton Archive/Archive Photos/Getty Images, p. 49; © Dave M. Benett/Getty Images, p. 51; © Qwerty Films/Warner Bros/The Kobal Collection/Art Resource, NY, p. 52; © Graham Turner/The Guardian, p. 53 (inset); The Granger Collection, New York, pp. 54-55 (bottom); © Laura Westlund/Independent Picture Service, pp. 58-59. Front cover: © Aaron Foster/Photographer's Choice/Getty Images (UFO); © Buriy/Dreamstime.com (forest); © Dmitriy Karelin/Dreamstime.com (starry sky). Back cover: © Glazyuk/Dreamstime.com.